SHOWTIME
READERS

The Canterville Ghost

Oscar Wilde

retold by
Virginia Evans · Jenny Dooley

Express Publishing

Published by Express Publishing

Liberty House, New Greenham Park, Newbury,
Berkshire RG19 6HW
Tel.: (0044) 1635 817 363
Fax: (0044) 1635 817 463
e-mail: inquiries@expresspublishing.co.uk
http://www.expresspublishing.co.uk

© Virginia Evans – Jenny Dooley, 2006

Design and Illustration © Express Publishing 2006

Colour Illustrations: Victor © Express Publishing 2006

Music by Taz © Express Publishing 2006

First published in 2006
Second impression 2008

Made in EU

ISBN 978-1-84679-354-7

Contents

THE AUTHOR

Oscar Fingal O'Flahertie Wills Wilde was born in Dublin on 16 October 1854. His mother was Lady Jane Francesca Wilde, a well-known poet and journalist, and his father was Sir William Wilde, a talented writer as well as a doctor. He had an older brother, William, and a younger sister, Isola.

Oscar was a very good student. He was clever, and he enjoyed writing. He studied at Trinity College, Dublin, and at Oxford University in England. When he finished university, Oscar moved to London, and wrote his first book of poetry in 1881. He then became an art reviewer and he travelled to America, Canada and Paris and gave lectures on art. Oscar also wrote reviews and articles for magazines and newspapers. He later became the editor of a magazine.

In 1884, he met Constance Lloyd in London. They married and had two sons, Cyril and Vyvyan. It was for his sons that he wrote a collection of fairy tales called *The Happy Prince and Other Tales* in 1888. He wrote his first and only novel, *The Picture of Dorian Gray*, in 1891 and the next year he brought out more fairy tales.

In 1892, he made his first venture into the theatre with his play *Lady Windermere's Fan*. It was very successful, and Oscar became quite rich. He wrote several other plays, including *A Woman of No Importance* (1893), *An Ideal Husband* (1895) and *The Importance of Being Earnest* (1895), which were all very successful, too.

Oscar Wilde died in Paris on 30 November 1900, at the age of 46. People still perform and watch his plays today, and his stories are very popular. People remember him as a very clever, funny writer.

BACKGROUND INFORMATION

Oscar Wilde's mother was very interested in ancient Irish fairy tales and she passed this interest on to Oscar. It is not surprising, then, that he used to tell his two young sons fairy tales and fantastic adventure stories to keep them happy. He published many of them in a collection especially for his children. *The Canterville Ghost* was the first of Oscar Wilde's short stories to be published, in a magazine called *Court & Society Review* in 1887. It is different from other ghost stories because it is a funny story and it shows us that ghost stories do not have to be frightening.

Oscar Wilde travelled to America many times and he used his experiences of meeting American people and knowledge gained from his travels to create the Otis family in *The Canterville Ghost*. He also used his experiences to highlight the many cultural differences between Americans and English people in his story.

At the time it was published, *The Canterville Ghost* was very popular, and even today it is still a very popular story. It has been made into a play, a TV series and a film many times. It is often seen on television and in the theatre. It has even been made into a musical! The story has been translated into many languages and is enjoyed throughout the world by both adults and children.

THE PLOT

The Canterville Ghost is set in the beautiful English countryside near an old town, Ascot, which is famous for its horse racing. Here, in Canterville Chase, a beautiful old country house, lives a 300-year-old ghost from an old English family. The ghost is famous in the area and has frightened many people for years. He is proud of being a very scary ghost. However, things soon change when an American family comes to live in his house, and problems arise for the ghost right from the start.

The previous owner of Canterville Chase, Lord Canterville, warns the Otis family that an old ghost lives there, but they are not worried, as they don't believe in ghosts. The Canterville ghost tries to frighten the family. However, they are not afraid at all. The young twin boys in the family play tricks on him and laugh at him. Mr and Mrs Otis even try to help the ghost. They give him oil for his noisy chains and medicine for his ghostly voice. The ghost is very upset and depressed and he tries to think of other ways to scare them, but everything he tries fails. The Canterville ghost is very sad but then one member of the Otis family helps him in a way he never imagined.

THE CHARACTERS

THE CANTERVILLE GHOST

is a frightening character. He likes to scare people so much that they become ill. He gets very annoyed when people are not afraid when they see him. When people trick him, he plans revenge. Sometimes, he can be scared himself — of people and other ghosts. He is actually very sad because he can't go to sleep.

VIRGINIA

is a very caring person. She gets upset easily when she sees things that are sad or unfair. She likes to help people when she sees they are unhappy. She is very brave, even when she is going to meet the Angel of Death. When she gets married, she is very happy. She is very good at keeping secrets.

MR OTIS

is a very straightforward man. He has no imagination. At first, he doesn't believe in ghosts. However, when he sees the ghost, he starts to believe in them. When things are broken, he finds an easy way to fix them. He is fair, and he doesn't want to upset the ghost, as he knows the ghost owned the house before the Otis family.

THE TWINS

are young boys. They like to whisper to each other and plan tricks to play on people. When the tricks upset people, they think it's very funny. They laugh a lot when people hurt themselves. They are quite clever and they are good at making funny plans.

MRS OTIS

is a very healthy woman and she is never ill. She is straightforward, like her husband. She hates her house to be dirty and she is very upset when she sees blood on the floor. She loves her family and she gets very worried when her daughter Virginia is missing. She is very relieved and happy when Virginia comes back.

WASHINGTON OTIS

is very sensible. He can solve problems very easily. He doesn't believe in ghosts. He thinks there is a simple explanation for strange things. He loves his sister Virginia a lot. He is very worried when his sister is missing and he spends hours trying to find her.

MRS UMNEY

is a very organised lady. She works very hard at Canterville Chase. She believes in the ghost and she is very frightened of him. She is so scared that she faints with fear. She is upset when the ghost dies and she wants to say goodbye to him.

LORD CANTERVILLE

is a gentleman. He is very honest. He tries to warn Mr Otis about his haunted house, even though he wants to sell it. He even allows Virginia to keep jewels that belonged to his family a long time ago, because the ghost wanted her to have them.

THE DUKE OF CHESHIRE

loves Virginia very much. He is very happy when he marries Virginia and he doesn't mind when he knows she is keeping a secret from him about the ghost. He is happy that she loves him. He knows that he will love her for ever.

1. The Warning

When the American Minister, Mr Hiram B Otis, bought the large old house called Canterville Chase, everyone told him that he was very foolish. Even Lord Canterville, who wanted to sell the house, tried to tell Mr Otis that it was a mistake to buy it.

"I must be honest with you, Mr Otis," said Lord Canterville. "There is something very strange about this house. My family and I don't stay here very often."

"But what is so strange about the place?" asked Mr Otis.

"There is a ghost here," said Lord Canterville. "It visits anyone who lives or stays here. My poor old aunt, the Dowager Duchess of Bolton, once felt two hands on her shoulders as she dressed for dinner. The hands were cold and hard, like the hands of a skeleton. My poor aunt was very frightened. She became ill, and she never really got better. That is why my family and I do not like to stay here any more."

"Did anyone else see the ghost?" asked Mr Otis.

"The Reverend Augustus Dampier also saw it," said Lord Canterville. "Dampier went to Cambridge University, you know. He's very clever, and not the kind of man who imagines things."

"No, of course not," said Mr Otis.

"After the terrible thing that happened to my dear aunt, most of our servants left the house and didn't want to come back here to work. My poor wife, Lady Canterville, could not sleep at night. She was frightened, and of course, the strange noises that we hear in the halls and in the library make us even more afraid."

"I'm not afraid," said Mr Otis. "I want to take the house, and the ghost. I come from a modern country, where we have everything that money can buy. There is nothing in Europe that we don't have in America. If there were ghosts, we would have some, too, and there are no ghosts in America, you know!"

Lord Canterville smiled.

"I'm afraid that the ghost is real," he said. "It is more than three hundred years old, for members of my family first saw it in 1584. Shortly before any member of my family dies, the ghost appears."

Mr Otis laughed.

"I'm sorry," he said, "but I don't believe in ghosts. There is no such thing!"

"Well," smiled Lord Canterville, "I hope you are happy in the house, but you must remember that I warned you, and you did not listen to me."

•2. Blood in the Library•

Mr Otis bought Canterville Chase, and a few weeks later, he moved into the house with his family. Mr Otis' wife, Lucretia, was a handsome woman and was always in good health. Their eldest son, whose name was Washington, was a fair-haired, good-looking young man. His sister, Virginia, was fifteen. She was slim and beautiful, with large blue eyes. After Virginia came the twins, who were lovely little boys, but they liked to play tricks on people.

It was a lovely July evening. The family enjoyed the evening sun as they travelled towards the house. However, as they got near to Canterville Chase, the sky became dark and big drops of rain began to fall.

An old woman stood in front of the house. Her name was Mrs Umney, and she was the housekeeper at Canterville Chase.

"Welcome to Canterville Chase," she said. "I have tea ready for you in the library."

The family followed her through the large hall into the library. The library was a long room with a large stained-glass window at one end. There was a dark red stain on the floor near the fire.

"Something has been spilt here," said Mrs Otis.

"Yes, madam," Mrs Umney said quietly. "That is blood."

"How horrible!" cried Mrs Otis. "I don't want blood on my floors!"

Mrs Umney smiled.

"That is the blood of Lady Eleanore de Canterville. Her husband, Sir Simon de Canterville, murdered her there in 1575. Sir Simon disappeared suddenly nine years later. No one ever found his body, but his ghost haunts this house. No one can clean the blood from the floor."

"That's silly!" cried Washington. "I can clean it up right now with Pinkerton's Stain Remover!"

He took a small black stick from his pocket and rubbed at the stain with it. The blood quickly disappeared.

"You see?" he cried. "I knew Pinkerton could do it!"

Just then, a terrible flash of lightning lit up the room, and there was a loud crash of thunder. Mrs Umney fell to the floor.

"What terrible weather they have in this country!" said Mr Otis.

"My dear Hiram!" cried Mrs Otis. "What can we do with a woman who faints?"

"We can take money from her wages every time she faints!" said Mr Otis.

When Mrs Umney heard this, she sat up. She was very unhappy.

"You must not make the ghost angry, sir," she said. "Terrible things happen in this house."

But Mr Otis and his wife were not afraid.

"We don't believe in ghosts," they said. "But we would like some tea."

11

3. The Ghost Appears

The storm continued all night long, but nothing strange happened, and the family slept quite well. However, the next morning, when they came downstairs for breakfast, they found the terrible stain on the library floor again.

"I don't believe it!" said Washington. "It must be the ghost."

He rubbed at the stain a second time, but the next morning it appeared again. That night, Mr Otis locked the library and took the key to bed with him, but the stain was there again the next day. The whole family were now quite interested. Even Mr Otis began to think that there might be a ghost at Canterville Chase, and that night he became completely sure.

It was a warm and sunny day, and in the evening, when it was cool, the family went out for a drive. They came home at nine o'clock, and had a light supper. They talked about famous actresses and actors, and about the foods they missed from America that they could not get in England. They did not talk about ghosts at all, and no one mentioned Sir Simon Canterville.

At eleven o'clock, the family went to bed. By half past eleven everyone was asleep and the house was dark. But suddenly, a strange noise woke Mr Otis. The noise came from the hall outside his bedroom and sounded like the clank of metal. Mr Otis got up, lit a candle and looked at the clock. It was exactly one o'clock. He felt very calm and was not at all worried. He could still hear the strange noise, and now he could also hear footsteps. Mr Otis took a small bottle from the table next to his bed. He opened his bedroom door and saw a terrible sight. There was an old man in the hall with red eyes and long grey hair. His clothes were old, dirty and torn, and there were chains around his wrists and ankles.

"My dear sir," said Mr Otis, "your chains are making a terrible noise. You really must oil them."

He showed the man the small bottle.

"This is a bottle of Tammany Rising Sun Lubricator," he said. "It's just what you need."

Mr Otis put the bottle of oil on a table near the ghost, then went back into his bedroom and fell asleep again.

4. A Terrible Shock

When Mr Otis closed his bedroom door, the Canterville ghost stood still for a minute. He was shocked. He could not believe his eyes or his ears. He picked up the bottle of oil and threw it onto the floor. He ran down the hall, making a terrible sound. However, as he got near the top of the stairs, a door opened, and two little boys appeared. They laughed and whispered to each other. Suddenly, they threw a large pillow at the ghost's head.

"Take that, you silly ghost!" shouted the twins.

The ghost disappeared from the hall in a flash of green light. The house became quiet, and the twins went back to bed.

The ghost found a quiet room in the house and stopped to think. He was very upset and felt terribly insulted. How could these people be so rude to him? Why weren't they afraid of him?

The ghost was more than three hundred years old. He was terrible to look at and he frightened everyone who saw him. The ghost thought of the Dowager Duchess, who became ill after he put his hands on her shoulders. He thought of the four servants who went mad when he smiled at them in one of the bedrooms. Then, he thought of the Reverend Augustus Dampier, who needed a doctor

after he blew out his candle in the hall one night. Also, there was old Madame de Tremouillac, who was ill in bed for six weeks after she saw him sitting in her armchair reading her diary. He remembered all the people who had seen him at Canterville Chase, and how frightened he had made them. He felt very proud. He was the Canterville ghost! He was famous all over the country! No one wanted to see him, or to be in the house he haunted. And now, some foolish Americans were here. They gave him oil for his chains and threw pillows at his head!

"This is terrible!" thought the ghost. "People should not treat ghosts in this way! They should shake and scream. They should run and hide. They should leave Canterville Chase and never come back!"

The ghost decided that it was time to teach the Otis family a lesson. He wanted revenge, and he wanted to make them afraid.

For the rest of the night, the ghost thought and planned until he had the perfect idea for revenge.

• 5. A Plan Goes Wrong •

The next morning, when the Otis family met at breakfast, they talked about the ghost.

"I do not want to upset the ghost," said Mr Otis. "After all, this was his house a long time ago. I don't think it is polite to throw pillows at him." He looked at the twins and they started to laugh.

"However," said Mr Otis, "the ghost's chains make too much noise, and I cannot sleep. He doesn't want to oil them, so I think we must take the chains away from him."

For the rest of the week, however, they did not hear the ghost. They knew he was there, because the blood stain on the library floor changed every day. Sometimes it was dark red, and at other times it was purple. One morning it was bright green! The family thought that these changes were funny, and tried to guess what colour the stain was before they came downstairs each morning. The only person who did not enjoy the joke was Virginia. She was always very upset when she saw the stain, and nearly cried on the morning when it was bright green.

The ghost finally appeared again on Sunday night. Soon after the family went to bed, the ghost

tried to put on a suit of armour which stood in the hall. However, the armour was very heavy and it fell to the floor. The family heard a terrible crash. Mr Otis and the twins ran downstairs. They saw the Canterville ghost sitting on a chair. The ghost rubbed his knees and looked very unhappy. The twins started to shoot pellets at the ghost, and Mr Otis tried to hold them back.

"What are you doing, sir?" he shouted at the ghost.

The ghost was angry. He made a terrible noise, then ran to the top of the stairs and laughed a terrible, ghostly laugh. Just then, Mrs Otis came out of her bedroom with a small bottle.

"You sound ill," she said. "Please take this bottle of Doctor Dobell's medicine. It's just what you need."

The ghost stared at her angrily. He tried to change into a dog, but at that moment, he heard footsteps and saw the twins coming towards him. He made a strange sound and disappeared.

17

•6. The Otis Ghost•

The ghost was very upset. He stayed in his quiet room and did not come out at all, except to make a new blood stain in the library each night. However, after a few days he felt better, and decided to try to frighten the Otis family again.

That night, there was a terrible storm. The wind shook the doors and windows of the old house. The ghost was happy. He heard the family go to bed and he waited until the house was dark and quiet. Then, at midnight, he wrapped himself in a sheet. He went up the stairs and walked along the hall. He decided to scare Washington first, because he was angry with Washington for cleaning up the blood stain. The ghost waited at the corner of the hall outside Washington's bedroom. When he heard the clock strike a quarter past midnight, he smiled and turned the corner. Suddenly he screamed and covered his face with his hands. There was another ghost in the hall. Its head was bald and its face was round, fat, and white. It smiled a horrible smile, and a red light shone from its eyes. There was a sign on its chest, but the Canterville ghost was too frightened to read it. He

ran back to his room, falling over his own sheet as he raced down the hall. When he got to his room, he jumped into bed and covered his face with the covers. But after a while, he felt brave again. He decided to go and talk to the other ghost as soon as morning came.

"After all," he thought, "two ghosts are better than one. We can frighten the family together."

When the sun came up, the ghost went back to the hall outside Washington's bedroom. The ghost was there, but now it looked different. There was no red light in its eyes, and it did not look very frightening at all. The Canterville ghost touched the other ghost and its head fell off. He saw that it wasn't a ghost at all. It was just a kitchen brush, a sheet and a large turnip with a candle in it. He picked up the sign and read it. The sign said "THE OTIS GHOST. THE ONLY TRUE GHOST!"

The Canterville ghost was very angry.

"Those foolish Americans tricked me!" he thought. "How can I make them sorry for this?"

• 7. The Twins' Tricks •

The Otis family made the ghost upset and nervous. He stayed in his room and he jumped every time he heard a noise.

"I have to appear in the hall at night," he thought. "I have to make strange and terrible noises. I am a ghost and it's my duty. I must do it."

Sir Simon was an evil man when he was alive, but now he was dead, his ghost wanted to do his job properly. Every Saturday, he walked in the hall from midnight until three o'clock, but he tried not to let the family see or hear him. He took off his shoes, and he even took a bottle of Tammany Rising Sun Lubricator from Mr Otis' bedroom and oiled his chains. However, the family knew that he was there, and the twins played terrible tricks on him. One night, they tied a piece of string to the furniture on each side of the hall. The ghost tripped over the string in the dark and fell over. On another night, the twins put some butter at the top of the stairs. The ghost slipped on the butter and fell all the way down to the bottom of the stairs. This made the ghost very angry, so he decided to frighten the twins. The next night, he wore different clothes. He took off his head and left it in

his room. Then he went to the twins' bedroom. The door was not quite closed. The ghost pushed the door hard, and a large bucket of water fell from the top of the door and splashed all over him. The ghost was very wet, and very unhappy, but the twins laughed and laughed.

The ghost went back to his room and stayed in bed with a cold for the next two days.

"At least I didn't take my head with me," he thought, "so I'm not wet all over."

The ghost did not try to frighten the Otis family again. He still appeared in the hall once a week, and the twins still played tricks on him. Sometimes they put nutshells on the floor of the hall to hurt his feet. Once, they hid in the hall, jumped out at him and shouted "BOO!" But after a while, they did not see the ghost any more, so the family decided that the ghost was gone for ever.

The Otis family were wrong. The ghost was still in the house, but he was so frightened of the twins that he became quite ill. He spent most of his time in his room and often stayed in bed.

● 8. Virginia and the Ghost ●

The young Duke of Cheshire had come to stay with the family for a while and he was in love with Virginia and wanted to marry her. One day, Virginia went horse riding with the Duke. She tore her dress on a fence and went home to change her clothes. As she ran to her bedroom, she went past the ghost's room. She saw the ghost by the window. He looked very sad and Virginia felt sorry for him.

"Don't worry, ghost," she said. "My brothers are going back to school tomorrow. After that, if you are good, no one will annoy you."

The ghost looked at Virginia in surprise.

"How can I be good?" he asked. "It is my job to walk in the hall, to make a noise with my chains and to frighten people."

"Mrs Umney told us that you killed your wife," said Virginia. "Is that true?"

"Yes, it is true," said the ghost, "but it was a family problem, and it's no one else's business."

"It's wrong to kill people," said Virginia.

"You don't understand," said the ghost. "She was a terrible wife, and I don't think it was very nice of her brothers to starve me to death, even though I did kill her."

"They starved you to death?" cried Virginia. "Oh, poor ghost. Are you hungry? I've got a sandwich in my bag."

"No, thank you," said the ghost. "I never eat or sleep, but you are very kind. You are not like the rest of your rude, dishonest family."

"My family are not rude or dishonest!" cried Virginia. "You are dishonest! I know you took all the paints from my box to make the stain in the library! You took all the reds, then all the purple, and when they were all gone you used green!"

"Well, what could I do?" asked the ghost. "It is *so* difficult to get real blood these days."

Then the ghost started to cry.

"Please, don't be angry with me, I'm so unhappy" he said. "I want to sleep, but I cannot and I'm so tired."

"How can I help you?" asked Virginia.

"The only place where I can sleep is in the Garden of Death," said the ghost. "You can help me get there. You are sweet and good. You can ask the Angel of Death to let me sleep forever."

"I'm not afraid," said Virginia. "Let me help you."

The ghost took Virginia's hands. Suddenly, the wall opened up into a big black hole. The hole closed around Virginia and the ghost, and the room was empty.

•9. Sir Simon's Secret•

When Virginia did not come down for tea ten minutes later, Mrs Otis sent one of the servants to look for her. But the servant could not find Virginia. At first, Mrs Otis was not worried, but when it got dark, she became afraid. The family looked all over the house and garden, but they did not find Virginia. Mr Otis, Washington and the young Duke took their horses and rode around for hours. They looked in the village and in the fields, and they asked at the station, but they did not find Virginia. They returned to the house and ate dinner. No one spoke during the meal. They all thought about Virginia.

Then, at midnight, just as the clock struck for the twelfth time, there was a crash of thunder. The family heard strange music and ran into the hall. Just then, the wall at the top of the stairs opened up and out stepped Virginia. Her face was white and there was a small box in her hands.

"Where were you?" asked Mr Otis.

"I was with the ghost," said Virginia. "He gave me this box of beautiful jewels."

"Oh, my dear! We were all so worried," cried Mrs Otis.

"You must come with me," said Virginia. "I have something to show you."

The family and the Duke followed Virginia through the wall, along a secret corridor and into a

24

small room.

There was a large metal ring on the wall, with chains hanging from it. On the other end of the chains was a skeleton.

"This is Sir Simon," said Virginia. "He was a bad man, but in the end he was very sorry. His wife's brothers kept him here until he died."

There was an old jug and plate on the floor. Virginia pointed to them.

"Look how his hand is reaching out for food and water," she said. "The jug and plate were too far away for him to reach."

Now the jug was empty, and there was only a pile of dust on the plate.

Virginia fell to her knees beside the skeleton, and the rest of the family looked at the terrible sight in front of them.

"Now we know the ghost's secret," said Mr Otis. "What a terrible story."

"His sadness is over," said Virginia. "Now he can sleep."

"You are an angel," said the Duke, and he took Virginia's hand and kissed it.

10. A Funeral and a Wedding

Four days later, there was a funeral at Canterville Chase. The funeral started at eleven o'clock at night. Beautiful black horses pulled black funeral carriages. Inside one of the carriages was a black coffin with a purple cloth on top of it. The servants walked beside the carriages with lighted torches. It was an amazing sight.

Lord Canterville travelled from Wales for the funeral. He sat in the first carriage with Virginia. Mr and Mrs Otis were in the next carriage, and Washington and the twins were behind them in the third carriage. Mrs Umney was in the last carriage. She had spent fifty years in the house with the ghost, and he had frightened her many times. She wanted to be there to say goodbye to him.

They buried Sir Simon in the churchyard. Virginia put some flowers on his grave and her eyes filled with tears.

"Goodbye, Sir Simon," she said.

The next morning, before Lord Canterville left Canterville Chase, Mr Otis asked him to take the jewels.

"The jewels belong to your family," he said. "They are worth a lot of money, so you must take them. However, Virginia wants to keep the box. Can I give it to her?"

Lord Canterville smiled and shook his head.

"The jewels are Virginia's," he said. "Sir Simon wanted her to have them, and she must keep them. After all, we don't want the ghost to come back!"

So Virginia kept the jewels and wore them when she married the Duke of Cheshire a few years later. She became the Duchess of Cheshire, and she was very happy. The Duke and Duchess loved each other very much. After their honeymoon, they travelled to Canterville Chase to visit Virginia's parents. They stopped at the churchyard on the way, and Virginia put fresh flowers on Sir Simon's grave.

"What happened when you were with the ghost?" asked the Duke.

"I can't tell you, my dear Cecil," said Virginia. "Please don't ask me."

The Duke smiled.

"You can keep your secret," he said, "as long as I have your love."

"You always have my love, Cecil," said Virginia.

"Good," said Cecil. "Then perhaps one day, you can tell your secret to our children."

Virginia smiled and took the Duke's hand. They walked happily towards Canterville Chase.

Activities

Before you start

The Author

1 **Answer the questions.**

1 Where was Oscar Wilde born?
2 What jobs did his father and mother have?
3 What university did he go to in England?
4 What countries did he travel to when he finished university?
5 Who did he marry?
6 How many sons did he have?
7 When did he write his first book of fairy tales?
8 What was his only novel called?
9 What was the name of his first play?
10 When did Oscar Wilde die?

Background Information

2 **Correct the sentences.**

1 Oscar Wilde's mother was interested in Scottish fairy tales.
2 Oscar Wilde published fairy tales and fantastic adventure stories for his father.
3 *The Canterville Ghost* is a scary ghost story.
4 Oscar travelled to Australia many times.
5 Oscar thought there were many physical differences between English and American people.
6 The story has been made into a film three times.
7 The book is published in English only.
8 The book is enjoyed by old people and children.

The Plot

3 **Look at the words. How are they related to the story?**

• Ascot • horse racing • beautiful old house • old ghost • Lord Canterville • Otis family • frighten • twin boys • oil • ghostly voice • depressed • help

The Characters

4 **Who's ...**

1 frightening?   ....
2 caring?   ....
3 clever?   ....
4 straightforward?   a)   ....
                        b)   ....
5 healthy?   ....
6 sensible?   ....
7 organised?   ....
8 honest?   ....
9 in love?   ....

Episode 1

Before Reading

1 Look at the pictures and the title. How do you think they are related?

2 Which of these things can you see in the pictures?

- top hat • table • windows
- reflection • carriage • candles
- flowers • dressing table • carpet
- beard • chair • waistcoat
- chimneys • gown • perfume bottle
- tree mirror

While Reading

3 Read or listen to the episode and mark the sentences as *T* (true) or *F* (false).

1 Mr Otis is from Europe. ....
2 Mr Otis wanted to sell Canterville Chase. ....
3 Lord Canterville thinks there is a ghost at Canterville Chase. ....
4 The ghost frightened Lord Canterville's uncle. ....
5 The Reverend Dampier went to Oxford University. ....
6 The ghost is two hundred years old. ....
7 Mr Otis doesn't believe in ghosts. ....

After Reading

4 Discuss in pairs.

- Do you believe in ghosts? Why (not)?
- Why do you think some people believe in ghosts?
- Would you like to visit a haunted house? Why (not)?
- What do you think is going to happen in the next episode?

Episode 2

Before Reading

1 Look at the pictures. Read the sentences below. Tick (✓) the things you think are going to happen in the episode. Listen, read and check.

☐ The Otis family arrive at Canterville Chase.
☐ A man is there to welcome them.
☐ They go to the library.
☐ There is a stain on the wall.
☐ The housekeeper becomes ill.

While Reading

2 Read or listen to the episode and answer the questions.

1 How many children has Mr Otis got?
2 What was the weather like when the Otis family came to Canterville Chase?
3 Who met the family at the door?
4 Why is there blood on the library floor?
5 What does Washington do about the stain?
6 What does Mr Otis want to do if Mrs Umney faints again?

After Reading

3 Discuss in pairs.

- Why do you think Mrs Umney fainted?
- Do you think the Otis family are kind people? Why (not)?
- Why do you think Sir Simon murdered his wife?
- What do you think happened to Sir Simon?

Episode 3

Before Reading

1 Look at the pictures, and the following words/phrases from the episode. What do you think happens in the episode? Listen, read and check.

- another stain
- library floor
- the family talks
- noise wakes Mr Otis
- a bottle of oil

While Reading

2 Read or listen to the episode. Then look at this page from Mr Otis' diary. Correct the words in bold.

Tuesday 30th July

My family went to bed at **1) ten o'clock**. A strange noise woke me. The noise came from the **2) bathroom** outside my bedroom. I opened the bedroom door and saw a **3) beautiful** sight. There was an old man in the hall. He had **4) blue** eyes and his hair was long and **5) black**. His clothes were old, **6) clean** and torn. There were chains around his **7) knees** and ankles. The chains were making a terrible noise so I gave him a **8) bowl** of oil.

After Reading

3 Answer the questions.

1 Do you think Mr Otis is clever or foolish? Why?
2 Is Mr Otis afraid? Why (not)?
3 How do you think the ghost feels now? Why?

Episode 4

Before Reading

1 Look at the pictures and answer the questions.

1 What are the twins doing in the first picture?
2 How do you think the ghost feels in the first picture?
3 Do you think the ghost feels differently in the second picture?
4 What do you think of the room?

While Reading

2 Read or listen to the episode. Answer the questions.

1 What does the ghost do with the bottle of oil?
2 What colour is the ghost when he disappears?
3 What happened to the four servants after they saw the ghost?
4 What did the ghost do to the Reverend Augustus Dampier?
5 What does the ghost do for the rest of the night?

After Reading

3 Discuss in pairs.

- How does the family feel about the ghost?
- Do you think the ghost is scary or funny? Why?
- Does the ghost want to be on his own?
- What do you think the ghost will do in the next episode?

Episode 5

Before Reading

1 Look at the first picture. What is Virginia doing? How do you think she is feeling?

2 Look at the pictures and the title. What do you think is going to happen in this episode? Listen and read to find out.

While Reading

3 Read or listen to the episode and complete the text below with the words in the list.

- colour • armour • breakfast • polite
- medicine • shoot • noise

The Otis family talked about the ghost at **1)** .... They complained that he made too much noise but Mr Otis told the twins that it was not **2)** .... to throw pillows at him. They noticed that the blood stain was changing **3)** .... One day, it was bright green! On Sunday night, the ghost appeared. He tried to put on a suit of **4)** .... but it fell to the floor. The twins started to **5)** .... pellets at him. The ghost was very angry and he made a terrible **6)** .... Mrs Otis tried to give him some **7)** .... because she thought he sounded ill. Finally, he disappeared when he heard the twins coming after him.

After Reading

4 Discuss in pairs.

- Why do you think the blood stain is changing colour?
- How does the ghost try to frighten the family?
- If you were a ghost, how would you try to frighten people?

Episode 6

Before Reading

1 Look at the first picture. Why do you think there are two ghosts? Which one is the Canterville ghost? How do you know?

2 Look at both pictures. What has happened to the second ghost? How does the Canterville ghost feel?

While Reading

3 Read or listen to the episode and put the events in the correct order for the Canterville ghost.

- [ ] He sees another ghost.
- [ ] He knows the Otis family has played a trick on him.
- [ ] He wraps himself in a sheet.
- [1] He decides to frighten the family again.
- [ ] He touches the other ghost and its head falls off.
- [ ] He goes back to the hall the next morning.
- [ ] He runs away to his room.

4 Read and correct the words in bold.

1 The Canterville ghost stays in his **noisy** room.
2 The storm shakes the doors and windows of the **new** house.
3 The other ghost's head was **hairy**.
4 The ghost went back to the hall when the **moon** came up.

After Reading

5 Discuss in pairs.

- Why do you think the Otis family made the 'Otis Ghost'?
- Do you feel sorry for the Canterville ghost? Why (not)?

Episode 7

Before Reading

1 Look at the pictures. What happens to the Canterville ghost in this episode?

2 Which of these things can you see in the pictures?

- shield • candelabra • bucket
- spider • night cap • spears • puddle
- wallpaper • pencil • portrait
- baseball bat

While Reading

3 Answer the questions.

1 Why did the ghost have to appear every week?
2 Why did the ghost take oil from Mr Otis' bedroom?
3 What happened when the ghost tried to frighten the twins?
4 Why didn't the ghost get wet all over?
5 Why did the ghost stay in his room?

After Reading

4 Discuss in pairs.

- Do you think the twins' tricks are funny or unkind? Why?
- Imagine you are the ghost. What are you going to do now?
- Do you think the ghost will leave Canterville Chase? Why (not)?

Episode 8

Before Reading

1 Look at the first picture. Where is Virginia now? How do you think the ghost is feeling? Why?

2 Look at the second picture. Where do you think Virginia and the ghost are going? How do you think Virginia is feeling?

While Reading

3 Read or listen to the episode and mark the sentences as *T* (true) or *F* (false).

1 Virginia went walking in the woods with the Duke of Cheshire. ....
2 Mrs Umney told the Otis family that the ghost killed his wife. ....
3 Virginia offered the ghost a sweet. ....
4 The ghost used green paint to make the stain. ....
5 The ghost found it difficult to find real blood. ....
6 The wall fell down in the ghost's room. ....

After Reading

4 Discuss in pairs.

- Where do you think Virginia and the ghost went?
- What do you think is going to happen to Virginia?
- Do you think Virginia is going to come back?
- Do you think the ghost is good or evil? Why?

Episode 9

Before Reading

1 **Look at the pictures and answer the questions.**

1 What is Virginia carrying in the first picture?
2 Why do you think Virginia's family looks so shocked in the first picture?
3 Where is the family in the second picture?
4 Who do you think the skeleton is? What is it doing?

While Reading

2 **Read or listen to the episode and replace the words in bold with the following:**
Duke of Cheshire, Virginia, The ghost, Sir Simon, The skeleton.

1 **She** stepped out of the hole.
2 **He** gave me these jewels.
3 **He** was a bad man.
4 **He** kissed her hand.
5 **He** was reaching out for food and water.

After Reading

3 **Discuss in pairs.**

- Do you think Sir Simon deserved his punishment?
- How do you think the family feels now?
- Why do you think the ghost told Virginia his secret?
- Who do you tell your secrets to? Why?

Episode 10

Before Reading

1 **Read the title and look at the pictures. Do you think the story has a happy or a sad ending? Who do you think will get married? Listen or read to find out.**

While Reading

2 **Read or listen to the episode and put the events in the correct order.**

- [ ] Virginia says goodbye to Sir Simon.
- [ ] Mr Otis offers the jewels to Lord Canterville.
- [ ] Lord Canterville sits in the first carriage.
- [ ] The Duke and Duchess visit her parents.
- [1] There is a funeral at Canterville Chase.
- [ ] Virginia marries the Duke.
- [ ] Virginia keeps a secret.
- [ ] Mrs Umney travels in the last carriage.
- [ ] Lord Canterville gives the jewels to Virginia.
- [ ] Virginia becomes the Duchess of Cheshire.

After Reading

3 **Discuss in pairs.**

- What do you think happened when Virginia was with the ghost?
- Do you think the story has a happy ending? Why (not)?
- Which part of the story did you like best? Why?

1 **Who wrote The Canterville Ghost?**
   A Charles Dickens   B Oscar Wilde
   C Lewis Carroll

2 **Who left the house and did not want to come back?**
   A The housekeepers   B The cooks
   C The servants

3 **What is Pinkerton's Stain Remover?**
   A a big white stick   B a small black stick
   C a small pink stick

4 **What was Augustus Dampier?**
   A a reverend   B a lord   C a dowager

5 **What animal did the Canterville Ghost try to change into?**
   A a cat   B a dog   C a donkey

6 **What did the Otis ghost have for a head?**
   A a carrot   B a cabbage C a turnip

7 **What did the Canterville ghost slip on at the top of the stairs?**
   A butter   B oil   C water

8 **Where is the only place that the Canterville ghost can sleep?**
   A The Garden of Life   B The Garden of Death
   C The Garden of Marriage

9 **What did the Canterville ghost give to Virginia?**
   A a box of jewels   B a box of gold
   C a box of money

10 **How many years did Mrs Umney spend in the house?**
    A thirty   B forty   C fifty

Discuss in groups.

- Which is your favourite character in *The Canterville Ghost*? Why?
- Which character didn't you like? Why?
- Would you like to visit Canterville Chase? Why (not)?
- Do you know anyone who has seen a ghost? Tell the class.
- Can you think of a different title for the story?

Project

- Imagine that the story takes place today. Write a modern story about the Canterville ghost. Think about:
  - what the ghost wears.
  - where the ghost lives.
  - what the ghost does.
  - how the ghost feels.
  - what the family wear.
  - what the family think about the ghost.
  - what tricks the twins can play on the ghost.
  - how Virginia can help the ghost.
  - how the ghost can go to sleep.
  - Tell the class your story about the modern ghost.

CHAPTER 1

appear (v) = when sth can be seen suddenly

believe (v) = think sth is true

dress for dinner (phr) = put clothes on for the meal in the evening

foolish (adj) = silly

frightened (adj) = afraid of sth

honest (adj) = always tells the truth

imagine (v) = think sth is there when it is not

library (n) = a room where books are kept

member of the family (n) = father, mother, sister, etc

mistake (n) = sth that is not wise

modern (adj) = new and has the latest ideas

noise (n) = sound

servant (n) = sb who does work in sb else's house

shoulders (n) = area between the neck and the top of the arms

skeleton (n) = bones in a body

strange (adj) = not normal

terrible (adj) = very bad

visit (v) = go to see

warning (n) = sth to tell people sth is going to happen that is not very nice

CHAPTER 2

crash of thunder (n) = a loud noise in the sky in bad weather

disappear (v) = go away and cannot be found

enjoy (v) = think sth is nice

faint (v) = when sb is not conscious so they cannot see or hear etc

fair-haired (adj) = light coloured hair

flash (n) = sudden bright light for a short time

in good health (phr) = when sb is always well

handsome (adj) = good looking

haunt (v) = when sb who has died visits a place

housekeeper (n) = sb who looks after a house and the owner

lightning (n) = sudden bright light from the sky during a storm

murder (v) = kill sb

play tricks (phr) = do sth to sb that is a surprise and (sometimes) not very nice

remover (n) = sth that takes a mark away from sth

right now (phr) = straight away

rub (v) = press on sth while moving backwards and forwards

stain (n) = dirty mark

stained glass (adj) = glass that is coloured in a pattern

tea (n) = drink (usually hot)

wages (n) = money that is paid for a job

CHAPTER 3

actor (n) = a man who is in plays or films

actress (n) = a female actor

ankle (n) = area between the leg and the foot

calm (adj) = not worried

chains (n) = metal rings put together in a line

clank of metal (phr) = a sharp noise made by metal hitting metal

continue (v) = carry on

cool (adj) = between hot and cold

footsteps (n) = the sounds of feet when they touch the ground

interested (adj) = think sth is important

light supper (n) = a small meal eaten in the evening

lock (v) = close a door with a key

mention (v) = talk about sth for a small amount of time

storm (n) = when there is bad weather with black clouds, lightning, wind and rain

torn (adj) = fallen apart into holes

worried (adj) = when sb is unhappy because they are thinking about problems

wrist (n) = area between the arm and the hand

CHAPTER 4

blow out a candle (phr) = to stop a candle burning with air

diary (n) = a book where there is a blank page for each day of the year

famous (adj) = when sb is well known

feel insulted (phr) = when sb feels that sb has been rude to them

perfect (adj) = as good as sth can be

pick up (v) = lift sth up

pillow (n) = sth to rest your head on in bed

plan (v) = decide what you are going to do

proud (adj) = pleased with yourself

revenge (n) = do sth bad to sb because they have hurt you

rude (adj) = say sth that is not polite

shocked (adj) = very surprised

stand still (phr) = stay upright and not move

throw (threw) (v) = let sth out of your hand quickly so it moves through the air

upset (adj) = unhappy

whisper (v) = speak very quietly

CHAPTER 5

funny (adj) = makes sb laugh

guess (v) = say sth that might not be true because you don't know

hold back (held) (v) = stop sb from moving forward

pellet (n) = small ball of paper or other material

polite (adj) = not rude

shoot at (shot) (phr v) = send sth through the air very quickly so that it hurts sb

suit of armour (n) = metal clothes to wear in a battle

CHAPTER 6

bald (adj) = without hair

brave (adj) = when sb is not afraid to do dangerous things

horrible (adj) = very unpleasant

kitchen brush (n) = a brush with a long handle that is used to clean floors

race (v) = run very quickly

scare (v) = frighten a lot

shake (shook) (v) = move quickly backwards and forwards

shine (shone) (v) = gives out a bright light

sign (n) = piece of paper with writing to give information

strike (v) = when a clock makes a noise at a certain time

trick (v) = do sth to sb to make them believe sth that is not real

true (adj) = real

turnip (n) = a large round white vegetable

wrap (v) = to cover sth

CHAPTER 7

bucket (n) = large metal or plastic container

cold (n) = an illness when sb sneezes and coughs a lot

decide (v) = choose to do sth after you have thought about it

evil (adj) = very bad

furniture (n) = large objects you put in your house, e.g. table, chairs, beds

hurt (v) = cause pain

jump (v) = move your body up suddenly

nervous (adj) = frightened that sth is going to happen

nutshells (n) = hard covers on nuts

slip on (phr v) = slide on sth

splash (v) = when liquid goes on sth or sb in small drops

string (n) = a thin piece of material for tying things

tie (v) = twist sth into a knot to hold it onto sth

trip over (phr v) = knock your foot on sth and fall over

CHAPTER 8

difficult (adj) = not easy

dishonest (adj) = not telling the truth

fence (n) = wooden wall to mark areas

no one else's business (phr) = sth that other people should not be interested in

problem (n) = sth difficult

starve to death (phr) = not give sb food so they die

tear (tore) (v) = put holes in material

CHAPTER 9

angel (n) = a very kind person

hang (hung) (v) = when sb or sth is attached to sth and is below it

jewels (n) = stones to put in rings or necklaces

jug (n) = a large container with a handle for liquid

pile of dust (phr) = a small amount of dust that is high in the middle and slopes at the sides

reach out (phr v) = move towards sth to touch it

rest of the family (phr) = the others in the family

secret (n) = sth that only a few people know

wooden panel (n) = a flat piece of wood that is part of a large piece of wood

CHAPTER 10

bury (v) = dig a hole and put sth or sb in it

churchyard (n) = the green area around a church

coffin (n) = a wooden box that holds a dead person

funeral (n) = when people come to say goodbye to a dead person

funeral carriage (n) = the vehicle used to move the coffin

honeymoon (n) = a holiday for a couple who have just been married

keep (kept) (v) = when sb continues to have sth

torch (n) = a long stick that can be lit at one end

worth a lot (phr) = when sth can be sold for a lot of money

Script and General Stage Directions

The narrator's part can be divided between two or more students, if the teacher prefers.

The narrator(s) should be dressed in black, so as not to stand out too much during the play.

The narrator(s) should always stand on the left or right of the stage, in such a way that they do not interfere with the action or obstruct the view of the audience.

Characters: Ghost
Mr Otis
Mrs Otis
Washington
Virginia
Twins
Mrs Umney
Lord Canterville
Duke

Narrator(s): At least one student, dressed in black.

Scene 1
Part 1

SONG: A Haunted House

Something's strange at Canterville
Something's not quite right
With shadows moving on the walls
And noises in the night

CHORUS: *Never buy a haunted house*
That's the golden rule
If you buy a haunted house
You must be a fool

People live at Canterville
But not for very long
It only takes one ghostly laugh
To show them something's wrong

REPEAT CHORUS

❖ ❖ ❖ ❖ ❖ ❖ ❖ ❖ ❖

Narrator: When the American minister, Mr Hiram B Otis, bought Canterville Chase, everyone told him that he was very foolish. Even Lord Canterville, who wanted to sell the house, tried to tell Mr Otis that it was a mistake to buy it.

Lord Canterville: I must be honest with you, Mr Otis. There is something very strange about this house. My family and I don't stay here very often.

Mr Otis:	But what is so strange about the place?
Lord Canterville:	There is a ghost here. It visits anyone who lives or stays here.
Mr Otis:	Are you sure?
Lord Canterville:	Oh yes. My poor old aunt, the Dowager Duchess of Bolton, once felt two hands on her shoulders as she dressed for dinner.
Mr Otis:	Two hands?
Lord Canterville:	Yes. The hands were cold and hard, like the hands of a skeleton. My poor aunt was very frightened. She became ill, and she never really got better.
Mr Otis:	Did anyone else see the ghost?
Lord Canterville:	The Reverend Augustus Dampier also saw it. Dampier went to Cambridge University, you know. He's very clever, and not the kind of man who imagines things.
Mr Otis:	No, of course not.
Lord Canterville:	We are afraid to stay in this house. We hear strange noises in the halls and in the library at night.
Mr Otis:	I'm not afraid. I want to take the house and the ghost.
Lord Canterville:	You are a brave man.
Mr Otis:	I come from a modern country, where we have everything that money can buy. There is nothing in Europe that we don't have in America, and there are no ghosts in America, you know!
Lord Canterville:	I'm afraid that the ghost is real. It is more than three hundred years old.
Mr Otis:	I don't believe in ghosts. There is no such thing!
Lord Canterville:	I hope you are happy in the house, but you must remember that I warned you, and you did not listen to me.

❖ ❖ ❖ ❖ ❖ ❖ ❖ ❖ ❖

Narrator:	Mr Otis bought Canterville Chase, and a few weeks later, he moved into the house with his family.
Mrs Umney:	Welcome to Canterville Chase. I have tea ready for you.

Scene 1
Part 2

Mrs Otis:	Oh dear! There's a mark on the floor.
Mrs Umney:	Yes, madam. That is blood.
Mrs Otis:	How horrible! I don't want blood on my floors!
Mrs Umney:	That is the blood of Lady Eleanore de Canterville. Her husband, Sir Simon de Canterville, murdered her there in 1575. Sir Simon disappeared suddenly nine years later. No one ever found his body, but his ghost haunts this house. No one can clean the blood from the floor.
Washington:	That's silly! I can clean it up right now with Pinkerton's Stain Remover! You see?
Mr Otis:	What terrible weather they have in this country!
Virginia:	Look at Mrs Umney!
Mrs Otis:	My dear Hiram! What *can* we do with a woman who faints?
Mr Otis:	We can take money from her wages every time she faints!
Mrs Umney:	You must not make the ghost angry, sir. Terrible things happen in this house.
Mrs Otis:	Ghosts! Ha!
Mr Otis:	We don't believe in ghosts.
Mrs Otis:	But we would like some tea.

SONG: I Don't Believe in Ghosts

You can tell me stories
Of ghosts who walk the halls
But I will only laugh at them
For I'm not scared at all

CHORUS: *I simply don't believe in ghosts*
And really, nor should you!
How can something scare you
When you know that it's not true?

Spiders give me nightmares
And snakes can make me scream
But ghosts can never scare me
For they're no more than a dream

REPEAT CHORUS

Scene 2
Part 1

Narrator:	The Otis family didn't believe in ghosts, but the ghost was determined to change their minds.
Washington:	Father, every morning, when I come down for breakfast, the stain is on the library floor again.
Mr Otis:	The stain?
Washington:	Yes, the blood stain. I clean it every day, and every night it comes back.
Mr Otis:	Never mind, son. It's just dirt. Good night.
Washington:	Good night, father.
Mr Otis:	My dear sir, your chains are making a terrible noise. You really must oil them. This is a bottle of Tammany Rising Sun Lubricator. It's just what you need.
Twins:	Take that, you silly ghost!
Ghost:	This is terrible! People should not treat ghosts in this way! They should shake and scream. They should run and hide. They should leave Canterville Chase and never come back! Why aren't they afraid?

❖ ❖ ❖ ❖ ❖ ❖ ❖ ❖ ❖

Scene 2
Part 2

Narrator:	The next night, after the family went to bed, the ghost tried to put on a suit of armour which stood in the hall. However, the armour was very heavy and it fell to the floor.
Mr Otis:	What are you doing, sir?
Twins:	It's the silly ghost! Let's shoot him! Pow! Pow!
Ghost:	Ahahahahaha!
Mrs Otis:	You sound ill. Please, take this bottle of Doctor Dobell's medicine. It's just what you need.
Ghost:	Argh!

❖ ❖ ❖ ❖ ❖ ❖ ❖ ❖ ❖

SONG: Respect

A ghost should be well-respected
People should run in fear
People should shake and shiver
Whenever a ghost comes near

CHORUS: *Why can't they just respect me?*
          I'm terrible and I'm bad
          They tease me when they should fear me
          It makes me so very sad

A ghost should be free to frighten
To rattle and moan and sigh
People should fear my hauntings
Children should scream and cry

REPEAT CHORUS

❖ ❖ ❖ ❖ ❖ ❖ ❖ ❖ ❖

Scene 3
Part 1

Narrator:	The ghost was very upset. He stayed in his room and didn't come out, except to make a new blood stain in the library each night. But one night, there was a terrible storm.
Ghost:	A storm! Tonight is the night! It is time to frighten those stupid Americans! First, I must frighten that boy who keeps cleaning up the blood stain! Aaaaagh! What's that?
Narrator:	After a while, the ghost felt brave again. He decided to go and talk to the other ghost.
Ghost:	Two ghosts are better than one. We can frighten the family together.
Narrator:	When the sun came up, the ghost went back to the hall outside Washington's bedroom. The other ghost was there, but now it looked different.
Ghost:	It's not very frightening at all. Oh! What does this say? "THE OTIS GHOST. THE ONLY TRUE GHOST!" Those foolish Americans tricked me! How can I make them sorry for this?

❖ ❖ ❖ ❖ ❖ ❖ ❖ ❖ ❖

Scene 3
Part 2

Narrator:	The twins played terrible tricks on the ghost. They made him upset and nervous.
Ghost:	I have to appear in the hall at night. I have to make strange and terrible noises. It's my job, and I must do it.
Twins:	BOO!!
Ghost:	AGH! Horrible children!
Twins:	Silly ghost!
Narrator:	The ghost was so frightened of the twins that he became quite ill. He spent most of his time in his room and often stayed in bed.

❖ ❖ ❖ ❖ ❖ ❖ ❖ ❖ ❖

SONG: Enough is
Enough

Those nasty twins are after me
It's just not fair, why can't they see?
I'm big and bad, I'm mean and cruel
But they just treat me like a fool

CHORUS: Enough is enough, I can't work here
They only laugh, they feel no fear
What can I do if I can't scare?
Why don't these people seem to care?

Before they came I had it made
The Cantervilles were so afraid
But now these people laugh at me
I'm just as sad as I can be

REPEAT CHORUS

❖ ❖ ❖ ❖ ❖ ❖ ❖ ❖ ❖

Scene 4

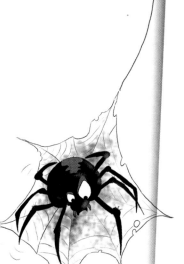

Narrator:	The young Duke of Cheshire was in love with Virginia and wanted to marry her one day.
Virginia:	I want to change my clothes before we go horse riding again!
Duke:	Of course!
Virginia:	Oh, ghost. You look sad! Don't worry — my brothers are going back to school tomorrow. You must be good until then.
Ghost:	How can I be good? It is my job to walk in the hall, to make a noise with my chains and to frighten people.
Virginia:	Mrs Umney told us that you killed your wife. Is that true?
Ghost:	Yes, it is true. But it was a family problem, and it's no one else's business.
Virginia:	It's wrong to kill people.
Ghost:	You don't understand. My wife was a terrible woman. And her brothers starved me to death! That was unkind, even though I did kill her.
Virginia:	They starved you to death? Oh, poor ghost. Are you hungry? I've got a sandwich in my bag.
Ghost:	No, thank you. I never eat or sleep, but you are very kind. You are not like the rest of your rude, dishonest family.
Virginia:	My family are not rude or dishonest! *You* are dishonest! I know you took all the paints from my paint box to make the stain in the library!

Ghost:	Well, what could I do? It is so difficult to get real blood these days. Oh!
Virginia:	Oh, don't cry! Why are you sad?
Ghost:	I want to sleep – but I need you to help me.
Virginia:	How can I help you?
Ghost:	You can help me get to the Garden of Death. You can ask the Angel of Death to let me sleep forever.
Virginia:	I'm not afraid. Let me help you.

SONG: Let Me Help You

We all need someone to care
When times are bad or life's unfair
When you don't know what to do
You know that I am here for you

CHORUS: *Let me help you, don't be sad*
Nothing's really quite that bad
All you needed was a friend
And now your pain is at an end

Hold my hand and come with me
I can help you to be free
All your sorrow's in the past
And you can go to sleep at last

REPEAT CHORUS

**Scene 5
Part 1**

Narrator:	The Otis family couldn't find Virginia, and they were very worried. Then, at midnight, they heard a strange noise in the hall.
Mrs Otis:	It's Virginia! Thank goodness!
Mr Otis:	Where were you?
Virginia:	I was with the ghost. He gave me these jewels.
Mrs Otis:	Oh, my dear! We were all so worried!
Virginia:	You must come with me. I have something to show you.

**Scene 5
Part 2**

Mr Otis:	My word! It's a secret room!
Twins:	Look! A skeleton!
Virginia:	This is Sir Simon. He was a bad man, but in the end he was very sorry. His wife's brothers kept him here until he died.

Duke:	Look how his hand is reaching out for food and water. The jug and plate were too far away for him to reach.
Mr Otis:	Now we know the ghost's secret. What a terrible story!
Virginia:	His sadness is over. Now he can sleep.
Duke:	You are an angel.

❖ ❖ ❖ ❖ ❖ ❖ ❖ ❖ ❖

SONG: Secrets

Secrets are like treasure
Precious things to hide
Do you tell your secrets
Or keep them all inside?

CHORUS: *We all have our secrets*
The things we never say
We keep them all inside us
Each and every day

Secrets can be painful
They make sadness grow
Sometimes we need to share them
To let our sadness go

REPEAT CHORUS

❖ ❖ ❖ ❖ ❖ ❖ ❖ ❖ ❖

Scene 6

Narrator:	Four days later, there was a funeral at Canterville Chase. Lord Canterville came from Wales.
Lord Canterville:	Well, well! The Canterville Ghost is gone.
Mr Otis:	These jewels belong to your family. They are worth a lot of money, and you must take them.
Lord Canterville:	No, no. These jewels are Virginia's. Sir Simon wanted her to have them, and she must keep them.
Virginia:	Thank you, Lord Canterville.
Duke:	You can wear the jewels when we get married, Virginia. What do you say?
Virginia:	Oh, Cecil! I'd love to!
Narrator:	So Virginia became the Duchess of Cheshire. The Duke and Duchess loved each other very much, and they lived happily ever after at Canterville Chase.

❖ ❖ ❖ ❖ ❖ ❖ ❖ ❖ ❖

*SONG: A Happy
Ending*

Sir Simon is at peace now
His story's at an end
He told the world his secret
And found a loving friend

CHORUS: *This is a happy ending
The story turned out right
The past is all forgotten
The future's looking bright*

Canterville is peaceful
A happy place to be
The house is full of laughter
And a happy family

REPEAT CHORUS

❖ ❖ ❖ ❖ ❖ ❖ ❖ ❖